Laughing At Myself

About all the times when life conspires to make you look like an idiot, and how to survive the embarrassment

Eden Gruger

© 2023 Eden Gruger
First Printing: 2020
All rights reserved.

Eccentric Girl Press

ISBN: 978-1-7398642-6-2

United Kingdom
https://www.edengruger.com

The right of Eden Gruger to be identified as the author of this work has been asserted by him in accordance with the Copyright, Designs and Patents Act 1988.

All rights reserved, no part of this publication may be reproduced, stored in or introduced into a retrieval system, or transmitted, in any form, or by any means (electronic, mechanical, photocopying, recording or otherwise) without the prior written permission of the publisher. Any person who does any unauthorised act in relation to this publication may be liable to criminal prosecution and civil claims for damages.

Book design by Sarah E. Holroyd (https://sleepingcatbooks.com)

For my funny ole Mum, who didn't get to see this book come out.

I would like to thank the real-life members of my family, friends, others and the universe, memories of, and about whom have helped inspire this book.

Having said you inspire me, any and all items with a factual basis have either been changed, (re-)invented, altered or included for expressive use (and as a necessary component of the relevant story).

That means that as a fictionalised work, no person or event depicted is to be taken as fact, as they are not. Any offence or displeasure is unintended, and I would be very sorry should you think that my characters are you. Or that events are a factual representation of anything that has happened.

Contents

River Island Trousers	1
Couch Potatoes	7
First Driving Test	11
Wheel of (Mis)fortune	15
Poodle Perm	22
Coke Burp	27
Bad Neighbour	30
Put Them Away Love	32
Mud Pack	34
Sexy Boots and Fishing Socks	37
Nice to See You	43
The Cat's Pyjamas	47
Cataract Toilet	50
Death by Frisbee	57
The World's Worst Burglar	60
Mensa Test	63
The Countryside is/not a Toilet	66
Flashing the Doctor	68

River Island Trousers

I was thirteen the very first time that I officially saw a boy outside of school, although, I wouldn't have called it an actual date. Least of all to my parents who were of the highly strung, control freak variety. They had wanted me to avoid all boys until my exams were finished, anyone who has read Down With Frogs will know how well that worked out long term.

Anyway, the boy in question was Christian Blake, a nerd, many, many years before nerds became fashionable. With his bowl cut, pristine school uniform, excellent manners, and timid little voice. I am still not quite sure how this outing came to be, as he couldn't possibly have asked me out.

Christian and his family lived in the same area of town as us, but in the next, slightly nicer road along from ours. Although we didn't know the Blake's as such, my dad somehow knew Christian's dad enough to raise a hand in greeting to him when their paths crossed. Which was, and probably still is, the equivalent of a full conversation for lots of dads.

Because even that raised hand was too close for comfort as far as I was concerned, I suggested that we met in the garages at the far end of my street. That way my Mum wouldn't be able to see us and drag me home if she just happened to be hovering behind her net curtains, which she was bound to be.

This was at a time before sartorial elegance and poise in teenagers had begun, a time before internet make up tutorials. When only grownups had cameras, and mobile phones were unheard of. So, I went to meet Christian with my hair in the same scraped up ponytail I had worn all day at school. Devoid of makeup, and wearing - I mean seriously picture this - an oversized orange and black Egyptian print t-shirt, black leggings and black school plimsols. I am still cringing now.

After meeting, we wandered around barely speaking, through the back streets to a playground, another cunning ploy to avoid parental eyes. And to show how totally past all this childish stuff we were, we pushed ourselves sarcastically on the swings. I hear you wondering 'exactly how do you swing sarcastically?' by looking as bored as you possibly can, going in circles rather than back and forth. And

Laughing At Myself

dragging your feet along the floor, of course, try it, you'll be amazed how cool you feel. I think we spoke about people we knew from school, I revealed with no prompting at all which girls fancied which boys. Girl code went well and truly out the window, sorry but I needed something to say, and I had literally nothing going on.

Once the entertainment of the park had been exhausted, we walked around the streets a bit more. And ended up at what we called the back river, but which was actually part of a drainage system, ahh the romance of it.

The back river looked like any other thin, slow flowing river, except that at one point concrete sloped down from each bank towards the middle. The slopes had a small channel between them for water to pass. The purpose of which must have been to slow the flow of waste water in the event of heavy rain. The local kids had always played there, jumping the gap over what was sometimes a trickle, and sometimes over what we perceived as boiling rapids. It does make me wonder how computer games caught on when all this excitement was to be had in real life, but there you go.

The grown up me can see just how irresponsible we were, given that only one child that I knew of could swim properly. One of the towns primary schools had a pool, but only gave a lesson twice a term, which wasn't going to help anyone become a great swimmer. The senior schools only gave swimming lessons to the boys, and no, I am not making that up.

Anyway, on this occasion the little channel was hidden under about a foot of water that was sitting in, rather than flowing through the gap. Thick with brown sludge it had been stagnant long enough for slimy strands of algae to start wiggling at the edges.

Of course, when I suggested jumping across the channel to Christian he reacted with a good boy's horror. Quietly pointing out his nice shiny shoes (shoes people, not trainers), and said that he didn't want to get them all dirty. When cajoling or teasing didn't work, I became sure that what he needed to make him want to join in, was to see me having the time of my life. The more he rejected the idea the more enthusiastic it made me, and the more sure I was that it would make him try. It is fair to say that I was an arse like this.

Running down the slope, laughing loudly to emphasise just how much fun I was having, and how free I felt, arms swinging, I jumped. I made it across the gap, landing with the delicacy of a fairy elephant on the other side. Giggling I waved from three feet, but in

Laughing At Myself

joy terms a world away, Christian looked unmoved. So over I went again, and again, and again.

All this jumping had gone to my head, and I was more than a little high on my showing off. Which made me want to show off even more, I needed to do something riskier. Something so daring that it had never been talked of, let alone seen. You'll never believe what I came up with, standing with my back to the water I closed my eyes and did a straight leap up and over.

You'd be right in thinking that this did not work quite as I had hoped, I did go up, just a bit. But with nothing to propel me, I also just went straight back down again, into the scummy water. Where I slipped on the algae, and landed with a cold, gloopy splash and a squeal, on my bum.

Being less than reasonable I was absolutely furious, I didn't dare look up at Christian, who I blamed completely. What need would there have been to try and impress him if he had been fun enough to do it? I fully expected that he would be wearing a smug, there you go. I knew it wouldn't be good for my shoes expression. And I couldn't bear it.

So, without looking at him I dragged myself out of the crud, and back onto the safety of the concrete slope. With the same spirit that has seen me through many trials and tribulations in life, I peeled off my soaking green and brown stained leggings and socks. And used my soggy tee shirt as a dress to get me home as modestly as possible.

Although he walked home with me, and I continued to chat, Christian didn't say anything, not a single thing about the incident. You won't be surprised to hear that we never met up again.

What my Mum said when I got in is unprintable.

Couch Potatoes

The house we bought needed quite a lot of work before we could move in properly, the elderly couple who had lived in the house before us were such heavy smokers that every surface had a sticky layer of tar that needed to be scrubbed off before any decorating could start.

But brown goo aside the house was a nice one, and one major plus point after our previous neighbours were the nice, middle aged sisters on one side, and lovely older lady on the other. The sisters had a large wolf-like dog which rocked the fence scarily as it tried to reach us, one of the first things that they ever said to us was 'he will bite, don't ever put your hands over'.

On the other side was a older lady who was so gran like we adored her as soon as we saw her, let's call her Miss Sweet. She couldn't wait to see what we did with the house, but was going away to visit her son for the first few weeks. We thought this was just as well, so she wouldn't be disturbed by our decorating noise and deliveries and whatnot.

The first step was the scrubbing, of everything from the ceiling down – have you ever washed a ceiling with a mop? If not, then I wouldn't recommend it. After that came the walls, woodwork, doors and windows, I don't think I had ever cleaned so much before, and I definitely haven't since. And that was before we could even start with the painting and decorating, even with help from friends and family it was a mammoth task. On more than one evening after a day of intense activity, one of us had sat down for a moment on the old sofa we found in the house, and had fallen sound asleep.

Eventually, the woodchip and our fingernails were gone, the Artex swirls had been replaced with smooth clean walls. The nicotine stains only lived in our memories, the new flooring was laid, the bathroom and kitchen were both bleached to within an inch of their lives, and all we had left to do was tackle the back garden at some point in the future, when time, energy and money allowed.

Despite it's rips and tears, its stains and general grottiness the old sofa had become a friend during the project. Apart from impromptu sleepovers, kids had played on it, or used it to rest on to do their homework while their parents helped us out. We had crowded on it to eat fish and chips out of the paper several times and had generally made extremely good use of it. So, we were pleased we still had it when Miss Sweet arrived with a box of biscuits, ready for a tour and a cuppa.

She admired all we had done and congratulated us on our hard work and being a lovely edition to the street. It would be fair to say we were glowing with her praise, it is amazing the effect that it has on people, have you noticed?

Miss Sweet began to tell us about the couple, who used to have our house. Mr and Mrs Neighbour had lived there for forty years, about how their children had grown up together, the times they had shared including times of need when they supported each other. Especially when ten years ago Mrs Neighbour had died.

Miss Sweet hadn't thought that Mr Neighbour would ever recover, but he plodded on, not really knowing how to manage without his beloved wife. 'You know how men of that age are', she ended her story with a sweep of her arm exclaiming, 'and it was ten years to the day we lost Mr Neighbour, he was right there on that sofa!'.

Eden Gruger

I don't believe we have ever moved so fast.

First Driving Test

Let's be quite clear before we start, I didn't feel ready to take my first driving test. My normal life anxiety was through the roof without adding in anything extra.

But I was very ready to be rid of my lecherous driving instructor, who I had booked ten non-refundable sessions with. It took less than half of the first lesson for him to start being overly complimentary, and from there on in he had spent most of our lessons making full on improper suggestions. Not helpful when you are trying to get the hang of changing gears smoothly. Every week he asked if I would meet up with him outside of our lesson, and my constant retort of 'will your wife and children be joining us?' didn't seem to put him off in the least.

Every night of the week leading up to the test I had actual nightmares, which really didn't help my confidence at all. It didn't occur to me that I could just cancel it. My legs were so shaky on my pretest lesson I felt that they might just bounce off the pedals, or not to be melodramatic about it, that I might collapse with terror before even getting out of the test centre. Looking back at what did happen fainting before getting in the car would probably have been the better (and safer) option for all involved.

The standard read the number plate part was easy enough, but all too soon it was time to leave the test centre car park. I drove carefully and competently down the very, very busy high road. It was (and still is) the sort of road where pedestrians like to cross over between moving cars rather than going to the zebra crossing. Despite that the first 200 yards were fine, in fact all of the first five minutes I was checking the mirrors and potential hazards like a pro. That was the first five minutes, and it went well.

No-one was at the zebra crossing as we approached it, so I planned to keep motoring slowly on. But as the car entered the zig zag lines before the crossing an old woman, complete with one of those little shopping trollies on wheels, stepped off the pavement.

Being fully versed in the Highway Code you will know without me telling you, that when there is someone on the crossing, and there is no central island, the driver must STOP NOW! So, as I was already on

Laughing At Myself

there, I had no option but to do a tyre squealing emergency stop.

The look of horror on the examiners face as he nearly brained himself on the dashboard, matched my own feelings exactly. I still have the image of the old lady turned to us with a look of utter shock and fear engraved on my brain. Hopefully this is what I have imagined since, rather than an actual memory, but we will never know for sure. My feelings have always been that despite the fact that she was probably someone's lovely old granny, and her own terror notwithstanding, that we should blame the old lady for this incident. And I feel that this must have been the view of the examiner, as he decided to push on with the rest of the test.

Wisely I think, he directed me off the main road to pootle around the side streets. As we rounded a corner a knee-high pile of builder's sand came into view on our side of the road. I told myself that it wasn't a problem at all, it was near enough to the kerb and easy to ignore. As my brain repeated 'avoid the sand' we drove over the mound and dropped back down the other side with a car rocking thud. It has been a constant source of amusement to me over the years that my brain freewheels like this, isn't it supposed to be helping me?

Eden Gruger

Neither I, or the examiner commented on the sand, instead he said, 'pull into the kerb please', and, no he didn't jump out and run away. In his same calm voice, he said 'When you are ready if you could attempt a hill start'. Attempt was the word, and when we rolled back a little, he advised me to use more gas, not that he thought I would use quite so much. We shot up the hill and over the junction at the top, mounted the pavement and narrowly missed the lamp post in front of us. Thank goodness no-one was coming.

All things considered, you could say that it was a show of driving skill to miss the lamp post and get the car back on the road. Unfortunately, a combination of oversteering and acceleration took us back across to the left-hand side of the road (where we were supposed to be). But it didn't stop there, we bounced up the kerb onto the pavement, narrowly missed the lamp post on that side, before leaving the pavement for the final time and coming to a stop.

It was at this point I believe that the examiner knew he was beaten, and the poor man suggested we head back to the test centre. I am sure mine was the worst test he had ever been a part of either before or since.

He was very gracious towards me which I have always been grateful for, much less so to my dodgy driving instructor.

Wheel of (Mis)fortune

At my local secondary school there was no talk of going to University. Whether some teachers had a chat with some pupils, I don't know, but if they did it certainly wasn't with me. No-one in my family had been to university or had a degree then, it just 'wasn't us'. So, it was quite possibly seeing an advert on television that made me want to do an Open University degree, ahh the power of tv advertising – it works. I can't quite remember now what gave me the push from ad viewer to actual do-er, it could have been looking through the course options – in the paper prospectus (I know), that was sent to my house (I know) that fired me up.

Without doing the slightest bit of research into what a degree involved, how much it cost, or how much time it would take, I booked my place on the first year of an English Literature Undergraduate Degree course. You may think that this was at best dizzy, at worse irresponsible, but my brain just does these things differently is all.

Eden Gruger

This was during the dark ages where although the internet did exist, a lot of people still didn't have home computers, it's not like we were writing on slates or anything. So, Open University study groups met monthly for in person lectures, given by *actual human tutors*. Hilarious, learning by actually meeting our teachers face to face in the same room at the same time, really what were we thinking?

As part of most courses there were educational television programmes to watch. These were shown on very late-night television, giving two options, to stay up until the early hours watching and making notes, or dum dum dum record the programme on video cassette. Anyone who just said video what? needs to see me in my office at 3pm to write the line, 'I must not make other people feel old' one hundred times. Harumph.

Anyway, back to my course, after signing up and finding out the amount of stationery I would need, it all went on my Christmas list including the bit I was most excited about - a wipeable wall planner. By the January start date I was chomping at the bit, my wall mounted planner was poised to be filled with programmes, meetings and deadlines.

Hmm... the writing pads were beautifully papery smelling, and poised to accept my written notes, the

Laughing At Myself

binders waited for my essays, and there was a whole range of pens and highlighters, it was all so exciting (is it weird to get a bit turned on by stationery? no? good). Anyone who asks why we didn't use laptops join the queue outside my office, you'll be writing the line 'things were different then' times one hundred. You may be thinking that after all this preparation that I would be ready on the day, you would be incorrect.

Although excitedly counting down the minutes to our first session all day, as usual I managed to be late. And not that 'not early' kind of late, but actual late, where the clock hands are past when you should have been sitting down wherever you are supposed to be. Where everyone else has either started without you, or is impatiently scowling at having to put up with someone being so inconsiderate.

In my defence, although my brain fully understands the concept of time, it also nearly always underestimates the time it takes to do anything or get anywhere. Which is part of a divergent brain, and also a family trait and means that I am very used to annoying people, and explaining.

On this occasion I had left home with a good ten minutes before I needed to be there, and just had to drive to the college, find a parking space and find the class. I managed the first two with three minutes to spare, and actually congratulated myself.

This would have been fine-ish, however, reception was closed, and in its place was a whiteboard filled with codes and arrows. Many brains like codes, but mine does not. So, this wasted precious time while I found a human person to explain this jumble to me.

The person looked at me, her expression was pure exasperation, should you look it up in the dictionary there would still be a picture of this persons face with me in the background looking confused. Naturally enough she didn't enjoy speaking to idiots, and I plainly was the *only* person in the world who didn't know everything automatically.

Apparently, the jumble on the board showed the course code, building letter, floor number and door number of the classroom. It occurred to me then, as it has many times since, that there should be a law, anyone creating a chart or table must provide a key to explain them, but apparently it would be 'unenforceable' ha.

Taking the first flight of stairs at a run, I jogged up the second, and practically dragged myself up the third with help from the banister. As I passed whole floors containing corridor upon corridor of dark

Laughing At Myself

rooms, I wondered exactly who had decided that none of these empty rooms could be used? deciding instead to put my class in the highest room of the tallest tower. Totally illogical.

Not used to running even at that tender age, by now my breathing was heavy. And it was a hot, sweaty, and slightly dizzy young woman who made it to the door. I gave myself a little shake and burst into the classroom head-first all big smiles and apologies. It was only once I made it inside the room, stood up straight and caught my breath, that I took in the sea of unimpressed faces turned to stare at me. One of the twits even glanced from me to the clock and back again, it was 7:06pm people, just six minutes passed time, which had felt pretty darn good to me until then.

Not only did everyone look at least ten years older than me, but they had also been there at the right time. By right I meant they knew the rule that to be fifteen minutes early is to be on time, and to be on time is to be late. That was the first time I had ever heard that, and it sounded like nonsense to me, it even had the word early in it. The tutor pointed out the only empty seat in the room. Naturally she assumed that not being able to tell the time properly also meant that I wouldn't be able to recognise a free chair. I expect she thought I would perch on a table, or huddle against the skirting board.

Eden Gruger

As an obvious punishment for my tardiness the tutor indicated for me to start the introductions. Having all the sense of a Labrador puppy and again apologising to the group for being late, I gave my name and work status. Part time bakery assistant, which is a fabulous job if you like cake. And then attempted to lighten the mood by saying that the reason I had been late was because I had been watching the Wheel Of Fortune and hadn't wanted to miss the final prize puzzle, and laughed.

I don't think you will be surprised to hear that this was met with stony silent faces. I realised that not only had I misjudged my audience, but these were definitely not my people.

When the other's introduced themselves they said things like... 'Mother to a small boy' (that one has always tickled me, a small boy as opposed to a freakishly giant baby? Or did she intend to make it sound like her son was the male Thumbelina?). Was being mum to a specific child more relevant than being a non-specific mum? You tell me.

Another of the gems was a fellow student who described himself, without even laughing, or blushing, as a 'multipreneur', good for you mate. You might get away with this now, but in the 1990s no-one said things like this.

Laughing At Myself

As my first experience of the 'take themselves far too seriously' brigade, it felt like a baptism of fire. After a few days of thinking it over, I decided to cancel my place on the course, I couldn't stomach three years with this crowd. Most upsetting for me, was not to be able to use the wall planner my sister had bought me for its true purpose.

It was another fifteen years before I would contemplate attempting a degree again, and by that time tutorials were only once every few months, with most things happening online. I had also learnt a lot by then about how to deal with the sort of people who go to great lengths to make themselves sound successful and exciting, by not giving even a tiny toss.

Poodle Perm

I went through a phase of being a regular at my local hairdressers, every four to six weeks. I would pop in for a quick trim and blow dry (just like the nice lady recommended). Which as well as keeping my split ends under control, would remind me just how nice my hair could look if only I could be bothered to style it myself.

This was at a time in my life before confidence allowed me to randomly chat to people that I wasn't related to. So, despite my regular visits you wouldn't have been able to say that my hairdresser and I had become 'friendly', and I blame this lack of confidence for what happened.

My hair had reached a length where it had started to get a bit flat and floppy, and definitely needed more 'oomph'. But not being au fait with curling irons, tongs or heated rollers, I chose what seemed like the easiest option to achieve a little height and texture. It was called a 'body perm', described as a light open

Laughing At Myself

wave which added body to the hair without curl, it sounded perfect, don't you agree?

Despite booking with my usual lady when I arrived at the salon they said she was away on holiday, but that I was not to worry as they had fitted me in with someone else. I was not keen on a last minute replacement, but I gave myself an internal talking to, after all there wasn't any reason to be worried was there? they were all professionals, and I really did want my hair done.

Once in the chair I took my glasses off, and settled into an extremely soft focus world, while a young girl with a bleached Mohican flitted around my head with rollers that would make a pencil look flabby. She occasionally shouted over the blare of hairdryers 'magazine?' but I'd point to my glasses on the side indicating that I couldn't see without them, and then she'd go back to chatting with her colleagues, and I would go back to being patient and trying to trust the process.

Hours later I put my glasses back on and saw with horrifying clarity that I now had the tightest perm that anyone had ever had, living on my head. It had literally reduced my chin length hair to about a half an inch of fuzz. It was also dried out to the point of sounding crunchy which hair should never do. It was

Eden Gruger

like having dead coral for hair, and not in a good way, I looked like a walking merkin. I could not have looked more ridiculous, in shock, I paid, stumbled home, and was greeted with my Mum's tactful 'what the f**k have you done to your hair?'

Would you be shocked to hear that this did not help me to feel any better? and summoning all my courage I phoned the shop to complain. The lady on the phone who wasn't my hairdresser or Mohican girl, said that she was aware of my appointment and that the lady who had 'looked after me' was at college that day (another red flag). This one said 'perms can be a little drying, it just needs a deep condition'.

She suggested a wax conditioner, which I attempted to buy in several shops without success and decided that it must be the hairdressers equivalent of tartan paint for when they want to get rid of an annoying customer, like one whose hair they've ruined.

At my mum's prodding I went back to see the manager the following day. She looked me straight in the eye and said she thought it looked really nice, full marks to her for keeping a straight face. She called various colleagues over to join us, who also said how pretty it was, and tried to convince me it was all ok really. How funny that as they all loved it so much none of them had an obsessively tight perm themselves.

Laughing At Myself

The manager didn't offer an explanation, an apology, a partial refund or a treatment to rescue the condition of my hair. Although she did offer to shave my head so that I could start again, which was nice of her.

At the shops and other places that I went to I wore a woolly hat. Sadly at work there was a definite no hat policy, and I had to brave the teasing and laughing behind my back. More than once I willed the floor to open and swallow me, sadly it never did. Over the weeks I became almost, not quite but almost immune to people's sideways looks of horror, mirth, and confusion, until I caught sight of my reflection, and was mortified all over again.

Then one evening while hiding at home John Frieda popped up in the ad break and told me something that would change my life (again). He had invented something that would transform dull frizz prone hair instantly. Ladies and gentlemen Frizz Ease had been invented, I could hear the angels singing.

The next day I was at the shop before they even opened to get the magic vials that would make me look, and feel human again. The day passed in a blur of excitement, I could not wait to rush back home to wash and restyle my hair. Occasionally I would fall into a mini despair that John may have been overselling the dream, and that felt like too much to bear.

Eden Gruger

It took me two hours that evening to apply the lotions in the correct order and blow dry my mop straight. But when I was finished joy of joys as well as arm ache, I had managed to turn my hair from crunchy poodle to shiny Lego helmet hair, which at least gave me another option.

And yes, I did change hairdresser, and I also learnt to be much less invested in other people's opinions after this.

Coke Burp

The first time I had an interview for a secretarial job I didn't actually get it, which was probably due to my complete lack of experience. But when the lady who did get it had to give two months notice to her current company, I was offered the chance to temp and get some training. I know a great chance when I see one and grabbed it. You may be impressed to hear that I tried my very best to show up early and was always late to leave. And in the time in between I worked twice as hard as everyone else, I wanted to absorb as much as possible in those few weeks and get a good reference.

My second impression must have been much better, as on the third week I was invited to an external meeting. Which the other staff said no-one other than management ever went to, this was exciting enough, but then I found out that my manager would be driving us *in his sports car*. My first ever business meeting, and first ever ride in a sports car on the same day, heady stuff indeed.

Eden Gruger

During the morning I did my best Duracell bunny impression, dashing here and there and generally being impressive. My energy must have rubbed off on my boss, as by the time we were due to leave his usual stern mood had loosened up. And he started sharing funny stories about the people we were about to meet. We stepped out onto a freezing November afternoon, whose light was already getting fuzzy, and climbed into his car. As the engine purred to life, I was introduced to one of the great joys in life, the heated seat. Would I like a warm bum? Yes please.

As a small town working class girl, my mind was already blown by this point, and then I noticed the multi-CD player. No-one that I knew even had one of these in their house let alone in their car. To save you youngsters looking it up, a CD or compact disc was a small disc that held music, and there was a time when it was quite the thing let me tell you.

I chuckled along with my boss's story very pleased to be getting the opportunity to win even more brownie points with him. Stopping to get fuel he came back with a couple of cans and had treated me to some chocolate, this was a truly amazing day.

Smiling my smuggest smile at the cold bummed pedestrians that we passed I took a large mouthful of super cold, super fizzy drink. My boss continued

Laughing At Myself

his entertaining monologue, and chose that exact moment to share a particularly hilarious if somewhat indiscreet tidbit. And Karma chose this moment to teach me not to be smug.

I tried to laugh with my mouth clamped shut, but this made me choke, and in the resulting coughing fit I spat fizzy pop all over myself, and the passenger side of his beautiful car.

Eventually regaining control of my lungs, I turned to him wide eyed with horror. It was at that moment the carbonation and coughing worked their magic and I released a massive lip wobbling burp in his direction.

The look of undiluted disgust he gave me was a slap in the face. Despite having been brought up well enough to know my manners, that look and the smashing down of all my efforts to impress caused my brain to spasm. And instead of saying 'Pardon Me' and having the good grace to vanish in a puff of sweet smelling smoke, I heard myself say 'Wow! that was a good one'.

If you have never had the sort of experience that made you want to disown yourself from pure embarrassment – seriously, you haven't lived.

Bad Neighbour

It was being quite tipsy at my housewarming party, that made being dared to streak down my new garden and back seem hilarious. Yes, my friends were of the bad influence variety. No-one has ever admitted being the originator of the streaking idea, or been able to explain how it gained popularity so quickly, but someone did, and then it did.

My garden was just a long lawn, with a chicken wire fence, and as well as the next-door houses, the ones in the next road also backed onto our gardens. Everyone had the same low open fencing, so there was zero privacy for such a stupid endeavour. Not like that felt like any sort of issue at the time. In the dark their windows seemed a long, long way off, and I felt sure no-one would actually see me at that time of night.

My wobbly schnapps addled mind reasoned that: it was night-time, and really dark. That not having met any of my neighbours no-one would recognise me

Laughing At Myself

anyway. And when they did finally meet me, they wouldn't be able to connect fully clothed in daylight me, with naked only seen for a few seconds in almost pitch black me.

Ever thoughtful my friends allowed me to negotiate keeping my trainers on, and with the formalities dealt with everyone gathered at the patio doors, I stripped off and with a bellowed countdown ran for it.

If memory serves me right, it was when I got to around ten foot from the safety of the door that the neighbours security lights began to ping on. Each seemed brighter than the last, until I was sure that it was lighter than day. My winter skin reflected, possibly creating a dazzling effect that made me invisible, but probably not. There was no point stopping so I ploughed on, laughing hysterically at full volume, as if not drawing enough attention to myself already.

How many of my new neighbours first glimpse of me was as an extremely tipsy, extremely naked, extremely noisy neighbour? I never found out but imagined many times the collective shaking of heads, and conversations along the lines of 'there goes the neighbourhood'. I promise I did try very hard to be a good neighbour after that.

Put Them Away Love

Jacob my boy friend, not my boyfriend, came from a very sociable family, hanging out with them was always a pleasure. In the summer we would usually be under the covered bar in their garden. As the weather got cooler the mini wood burner would go on, making the space cosy and welcoming. Before eventually the winter would push us inside to the real log burner.

Their family included two brothers, a sister, three eccentric uncles and several long-term neighbours. The younger generations had that shorthand of having grown up together, and a bond as close as any blood family.

Invitations weren't needed, and people would arrive as and when they wanted with their own friends and partners in tow. I loved it there.

Sadly, I managed to get myself permanently uninvited to their gatherings, it was a total accident,

Laughing At Myself

but I can sort of see why. After flashing my boobs at Jacob, the neighbour's thirteen year old son also got an eyeful, his dad thought it was funny, his mum did not.

Why did I flash Jacob in the first place? Shall we blame girl power? These are my boobs and I'll show them if I want to, the ladette culture? or my own silliness? I'll let you choose what feels right to you. But before you decide let me say that Jacob flashed his bum at me first, and no-one complained about that (to my knowledge).

I did attempt to explain and apologise to Jacob's Mum and the neighbour. And yes, I did and still do appreciate that the lad was standing right beside Jacob, right in front of me. And some would say why should he be subjected to my boobs? the first boobs he had ever seen in real life. But at the time I just didn't notice him.

Mud Pack

It felt like it had been raining non-stop for months but was only really a couple of weeks. We were so sick of being inside that the second the weather cleared up abit, the boyfriend and I headed out for the day. He had heard about a giant Buddha statue sitting on top of a hill, so off we went to investigate.

It turned out that the Buddha was about five kilometres from the car park, most of that across fields, which were now like wading through a swamp. Sloshy, sticky and slow going I was worried that I would lose at least one welly boot, but this was one of the times when the Gods were smiling on me, and both feet mercifully stayed dry.

Eventually with calf muscles burning, we rounded a corner and there he was, sat atop quite a steep hill looking down on us. Smiling and benevolent it was The Buddha, and he was massive. The landowners had kindly built a Chinese style pagoda at the bottom of the hill, so you could look up and admire him. And

Laughing At Myself

just as importantly catch your breath before tackling the hill, which is what we did for a while. There were quite a few other people who had the same idea as us, and as fast as people left their seats they were taken. Everyone sat quietly, some in awe of the sight in front of us, and some I think, because they were tired out.

By the time we arrived to sit on Buddha's lap we were pink cheeked and puffing but exhilarated. We took each other's photograph mirroring the statue's pose and spent several minutes in quiet contemplation of the peaceful atmosphere, and surrounding countryside before heading back down.

It was then that the sludge took the boyfriends feet from under him (yay it wasn't me for once). Down he thumped, and away he slipped, travelling a good few feet before squelching to a stop. The brief moment that followed was of the purest silence, which was then smashed by the peals of laughter that rang out from above and below us. It was a classic comedy moment, people chuckled from the top of the hill, they giggled as they came up the hill. The laughter that reached us from the pagoda far below just tipped it over into comedy gold. The boyfriend did not agree, he was fuming.

I did help him up, and check he wasn't hurt, and tried to make light of the mud that ran in a stripe from his boots, up to and including the back of his head. But an action replay ran in my head, and every time it played it set off an uncontrollable giggle, and that would create a ripple of others from all around us.

At several points of near clinical hysteria, I was bent double unable to move with tears streaming down my face. I would have expected, nay encouraged this reaction if it had happened to me. But he was not amused. What a stick in the mud.

Sexy Boots and Fishing Socks

The thing that had gotten muddled this time, was the date of Gemma's birthday party. Of course, I knew that it was coming up, but having lost track of the date I just hadn't realised that her birthday was the next day, not until someone called to check the time we were meeting.

Fortunately, the outfit I planned to wear was long settled, except for the shoes that is, none of my current collection went with my dress, wrong colour, wrong style, or just too scuffed.

With a late shift at work that day, and a morning shift the day of the party, it would be a struggle to find time to fit in some shoe shopping. But I was just going to have to try, luckily, I knew just the boots that were needed, unluckily that meant having to find them, going shopping knowing exactly what you want can be a horrendous pain in the butt. Anyway,

Eden Gruger

if I pulled some military grade time management out of the bag it seemed possible to find a spare half hour. All I had to do was find a parking space and run to the three shoe shops in town and find the exact boots that I wanted, so that wouldn't be even slightly rushed.

Some Ninja level parking got me a space, and to make sure that I didn't do my usual trick of forgetting the time, I set an alarm on my phone to tell me when to head back to the car. As I speed walked to the first shop, I visualised seeing the boots as I went in and being able to leave early and victorious, this didn't work. Not sure the three minutes between the car and the store was enough for the universe to hear and provide.

The second shop had a pair that were almost right, but the heel was too skinny and too high for me. On I rushed to the third and final shop, and my final chance for the right shoe. By now the universe had picked up, and there they were, in the window display, just waiting for me, knee length black boots with a platform heel. They were tall enough to make me feel sexy, but the level platform meant I'd be able to walk without too much wobble.

Attracting the eye of one of the sales assistants when they were mid gossip was no mean feat and no, I

Laughing At Myself

didn't manage it. In the end I had no option than to burst into their huddle and say, 'can I have those boots in the window in a size four please?'. They turned their black rimmed eyes to me with disdain, looking every inch like the school bullies they may have once been. Before you say anything, I am well aware that not all people who work in a shoe shop are mean, or women, or anything else, but these ones were, ok?

One of the assistants replied over her shoulder 'size six only', before turning back to her conversation. My response? 'I'll try them anyway', I don't mind telling you this got some raised eyebrows. One of the gang, not 'size six only' peeled herself off the glass counter and trudged over to get the boots out of the window display.

I could almost have put them on over my other shoes they were that big. Walking was fun, with my foot taking a step, and the boot dawdling behind at a two second delay, but that couldn't be a deal breaker. They looked right and my shopping time was almost up. I would just have to work around it, so I bought the boots.

The rest of my day I see-sawed between a smile that I had been able to find the right shoe, and puzzlement about how I could make them fit. In the end I decided the easiest and cheapest thing to do, would be to wear extra socks. Wearing enough pairs that my feet would be wedged into a somewhat smaller hole would surely make all the difference.

At 7pm all dressed up and ready to leave, the boots felt fine, striding from one side of my bedroom to the other, I just knew my sock plan was going to work. Walking to the station felt amazing, I was tall (or my version of tall), and my confidence knew no bounds. By the time I reached the station however, my feet had started to throb in what I can only describe as a cartoonish manner. Inside my boots they pulsed hotly, but that was inside my boots, from the outside they still looked great. It would be ok, I told myself these boots weren't made for walking, they were made for being admired, and that I could rest on the train, which I did.

Arriving in town and meeting up with Gemma and our friends chased all thoughts of sore feet away. The excited chatter, singing Happy Birthday, throwing confetti in the shape of mini champagne bottles over her head like the birthday bride, didn't leave room for anything else.

The two extra centimetres in each boot was quite determined to make their presence felt. And, on the short stroll from the pub to the club, they used them

Laughing At Myself

to trip over a virtually flat paving slab. This fall was nothing whatsoever to do with alcohol, it was the boots revenge. Obviously, the girls had no idea, and teased me about being able to get drunk on a wine gum. Someone handed me a tissue to mop up the blood from my grazed knee, and then a helpful set of arms hoisted me upright, gave me a hug, and we were off again.

Arriving at the club we did the customary reconnoitre (I have no idea why we needed to do this, but it had been a habit for years. We probably saw it on telly and thought it looked cool). Wandering through all the different bar and dance floor areas looking like we owned the place, we tried to give an air of being vaguely bored by it all. We hardly even bothered to look at anyone, but when we recognised someone they were showered with enthusiastic greetings and hugs.

Having chosen which would be 'our spot' for the evening (a seating area near, but not too near the bar, overlooking the largest dance floor, and not too far from the ladies), the dancing could begin. I tried, I really did, but after an hour my feet were nuclear, they needed a rest as much as the rest of me didn't want one, there was no option but to retire to our table. Sighing as I plonked myself down, it was time to admit it to myself, if I wanted to be able to move away from the comfort of the table the boots would have to come off.

My friends' shrieks of amusement almost drowned out the music when I unzipped and removed the boots. Revealing a pair of my dad's extra thick, calf length fishing socks, in camel. I simply cannot imagine why this arrangement had been uncomfortable. We all had a jolly good laugh at my expense, and I really didn't mind, it was a relief to be free.

Getting back on the dance floor again was painful bliss, I ignored the fact that people were giving me funny looks. When you do enough daft things, you eventually develop a thick enough hide to have a virtually non-existent embarrassment threshold. I may have looked deranged, in my obscenely tight mini dress, fishing socks and grazed knees, to be fair I was a bit, but that was nothing. Now I could dance the night away with my usual abandon. I like to think I made quite the statement, and still got asked to dance by a lad who was celebrating his 18th birthday (probably as a bet, but never mind, it still counts).

We walked home at 5am, me on red raw feet that would over the next few hours swell and be impossible to stand on for a few days. But fortunately, I didn't care about that by then, as I was very, very drunk.

Nice to See You

It will surprise no-one at all to hear that I had slept through my alarm, and consequently was running late for work. Or that although my stay at the boyfriend's house had been planned, this hadn't translated into me thinking to pack a change of clothes. No, I had mistakenly assumed it would be possible for me to get up early enough to go home and change. We all know that was never going to happen, don't we? So, there I was with no change of clothes and no makeup, and all the planning abilities of a goldfish.

Throwing on my outfit from last night, a pretty and just about work appropriate black blouse with floaty sleeves and black skinny jeans, I felt very fortunate that the office wasn't formal business wear, or I'd have been totally screwed, as it was this was seriously pushing work casual.

The boyfriend wasn't rushing, he didn't have to be at work until 10am. Turning to him in frustration I threw my arms wide and gave him a twirl, 'do I look

OK enough?'. He looked up over his toast and nodded yes, he never spoke before 9am, how he would have called the fire brigade had the flat been on fire is anyone's guess.

Once in my car and on the road the traffic was flowing nicely, I thought I'd be able to make up some time, and relaxed. Hungry after not having had any breakfast, but feeling better, by the time I pulled into my parking space I was ready to face the day with a smile.

My office was reached by walking through virtually every other department of the company. Starting with the loading bay, the workshop, packing and across the sales floor, before hitting the director's corridor. Rather than being a pain, this had always been my chance to check in with everyone, instead of being hidden in the office all day.

As I started my hello's the day seemed to have turned around, this was going to be a great day. Everyone was smiling and looked pleased to see me. The days when the whole team were feeling positive were quite rare, so I planned to make the most of it. There was a bounce in my step by the time I got to my team, and I threw myself into the mornings work. I hadn't even stopped for a coffee by the time people started to talk about elevenses, and a trip

Laughing At Myself

to the kettle and ladies was long overdue. On my way to the kitchen I popped my head around the director's door to offer him a coffee, before heading off to 'pay a visit' while the water boiled.

It was while I was washing my hands at the sink I looked up into the mirror and saw for the first time what my colleagues had noticed all day. In the bright overhead lights, my shirt was virtually see-through, and my lovely somewhat racy, lacy bra was on show for all to gawp at. Flashbacks of everyone's enthusiastic greetings fast forwarded through my mind. Folding my arms across my chest I hurried back to my office 'I'm going to need to pop home'. My manager raised a quizzical eyebrow until I opened my arms and gave her a flash. Although she sounded exasperated and rolled her eyes, she said I could go, and she lent me her cardigan to cover myself up.

Even now no-one could see anything, I kept my arms crossed until I made it to my car. One of the skills I had developed from being late so often was the ability to get changed super quickly. So, I was able to dash home and be back in my parking space in just under fifteen minutes. I would have been even quicker if I hadn't stopped to call the boyfriend and ask him exactly why he hadn't mentioned the bra situation that morning. His reply? "I just assumed you knew", yes you flaming idiot I always go to work with my boobs on show. Sigh.

I was teased at work for several weeks after that, with their favourite comment being 'when are you going to wear that black blouse again? We really liked that one'.

The Cat's Pyjamas

I was having a birthday party at home, and the guy that I was sort of seeing (Mr Don't Ask), had offered to DJ, which was very kind of him. And it had the added bonus of giving his neighbours ears a break for the evening. He had so much paraphernalia that he brought his friend with him to help shift it. I had only met the friend once, but he seemed like a normal sort of bloke.

From what I could tell a good night was had by all, not that I remember much of it. Most of what I know about the night came from the photographs, which showed a lot of smiling, happy people. After everyone had eventually left, my squeeze and me tootled off to the bedroom, leaving his mate to sleep on my sofa. This wasn't nearly as bad as you might think, as it was the world's biggest settee.

I bought it without measuring – I know, I know, and in fact hadn't planned to buy a sofa at all. While hiding from the rain an ever so lovely salesman charmed me. This thing was colossal, and took up a third of the entire room, so was very cosy for lounging around on, and sleeping visitors.

Too early in the morning we were woken up by a yell from the living room, that sort of thing will wake you up faster than any alarm clock. Jumping up I shouted at Mr Don't Ask to get him out of bed, so that we could both go and see what was going on. It sounded like a burglar had climbed in the window, and had landed on his friend, who was (verbally at least) giving it his best shot at scaring the intruder off. We dashed towards what had now become an absolute riot of ranting, what on earth was going on in there?

Bracing ourselves we flung the door open, to find him standing all alone in the middle of the room wearing, I kid you not, a pair of stripy pyjamas. In our house we know them as 'Colgates' after the famous toothpaste with stripes. I'm just going to put this out there, have you ever heard of anything so bizarre as taking pyjamas to a house party? Maybe you have but for me this was a shocker. He appeared to be shouting at the pair of trousers he held at arm's length in one hand, and a shirt that he had at arm's length in the other. My nose twitched, it was the smell that gave it away, 'did you by any chance shut the cat in with you last night?'

Laughing At Myself

Needless to say he had, but was unimpressed when I explained that elderly cats and closed doors, that separate them from their litter tray do not good situations make. The cat was sitting on the end of the sofa looking unimpressed, so I whisked him into the other room before he had a chance to do anything else. And yes, I did explain to him that it wasn't his fault (it really wasn't).

By now the bloke was making such a fuss that I offered to wash and dry his clothes for him before he went home. But having worked himself into quite a state he wasn't interested in being helped, insisting instead on going home in his pyjamas.

As he helped carry equipment to the car Mr Don't Ask and I kept catching each other's eyes and gesturing discreetly to his mate. I am not sure what it is that makes being outside in your night clothes in the dead of winter comical, but it was. He, of course did not see the funny side, and that just made it more hilarious for us, and the more cross he got the funnier it became. And yes, before you ask, I would have laughed if it happened to me. My dog once mistook me for a lamp post while we were on our way to the vets (he had a lot on his mind) and peed down my leg. I laughed my arse off then too.

Cataract Toilet

If you have ever been behind me in a queue for the ladies and wondered why I always lock and unlock the door before I close it. This will explain all.

Being the fabulous daughter that I obviously was, what else would I do when Mum needed to get to a check-up before her cataracts operation but offer to take her to the hospital and keep her company in the waiting room? This was her first time seeing the actual specialist to find out if her cataract was 'ripe enough' to operate on, I think this expression is gross, but it is the real one, so there we go.

We arrived with plenty of time to spare before the appointment so that mum had time to 'settle in'. Which translates into she had time to take her coat off, pop to the ladies, and then chat to whoever was in the waiting room for a bit. The chatting part was very important apparently, although my dad was still very much around, mum told me that after forty six

Laughing At Myself

years of marriage she really was in need of some fresh conversation.

Chatting happily to her neighbour, she asked about the woman's bus journey, and made sure to tell her that with me to help *she* didn't have to travel by bus. Cue a squeeze of my arm, and a smile that I only ever got in front of strangers. Now my part in the conversation (as mum's prop), was essentially over it was time to check out the waiting room reading material. It should not have been a shock to me that the eye surgeon's waiting room did not have a great selection of magazines. Not for anyone under sixty who didn't have an eye problem anyway.

Spreading the small pile of publications across the table showed a definite theme, there were a few copies of Optician magazine. And a couple of very tattered Eye Magazines, yes, they are both real publications look them up if you don't believe me. Other than that, there was of course the usual copies of Readers Digest, a leaflet about stairlifts, and one about a community home help service. It took barely a few minutes to flick through the magazines.

Then it was onto the various posters dotted around the peeling walls, they consisted of an absolutely riveting, and quite gross diagram of the eye. An advertisement for the previously mentioned community home help service, a large print notice about not eating and drinking in the waiting area. And my personal favourite, the sign about the zero tolerance policy for people being verbally or physically aggressive towards the unit staff, as they're there to help. I couldn't help thinking that the sort of person who would throw abuse or fists at staff, isn't the sort of person who would care what a sign says, but I suppose they had to try.

Fifteen minutes in there wasn't anything else to do, and the random chatty person that you always find in waiting rooms, the one who usually starts a conversation saying something like 'murder trying to get a parking space this morning,' or 'I think they are running thirty five minutes late by the look of things, my appointment was due at half past'. Who we, as a fairly polite nation of people feel duty bound to answer, had gone into his appointment at the same time as my Mum. Leaving just us, overly conscious too afraid to initiate conversation types behind.

I was getting quite mad with boredom and thought a trip to the ladies would get rid of a minute or so. But the door was right beside the seating area, and the thought of people being able to hear me made me nervous. I am one of those people who don't like to pee if there is someone in the cubicle next to me, so the thought of broadcasting to the waiting

Laughing At Myself

room was enough to put me off altogether. But, after watching several other people go in, and not hearing them doing anything, I presumed it was sound proofed enough. Pee complete, hands washed, and my reflection checked, I turned the lock and pushed down the door handle. But nothing happened, I tried again and again, but it wouldn't budge.

The second it became clear that I was trapped, my natural panic took over. I started to bang on the door but could hear nothing from the other side. I called out, but again nothing, then my frantic eye caught sight of the emergency pull cord – well wasn't this a case of emergency? It certainly felt like it, so I pulled the alarm. Someone would come and open the door from the other side, and freedom would be mine!

The volume of the siren was quite a surprise, as was the instantaneous taps on the door. A muffled voice called through the door 'are you conscious?' and I explained that although panicking I wasn't ill. On the advice of the voice I jiggled the lock one more time, and what do you know? It popped open. It was a hyperventilating, shaky me that sprung out of the toilet into the waiting crowd of doctors, nurses and sundry other medical people. And of course, the entire waiting room had turned to see the drama.

Eden Gruger

Apparently, the alarm sounded throughout the unit and that's why everyone had rushed to my aid. That was a lucky thing, as this time I really felt like I might die of embarrassment. As soon as they realised the excitement was over, and I had apologised, the staff disappeared back to their stations with a general air of disappointment. To make it even more fun, I then had to sit and wait for twenty more minutes, with everyone thinking I was a prize idiot until Mum came back.

And then there was the time that the new team I had joined at work went to dinner in a fancy French restaurant. They were celebrating a big contract that they had managed to bring in. All the work had happened before I actually joined them, so I was eating on false pretences really.

Wine flowed and there was an air of mutual appreciation around the table. Not only had they secured themselves some generous bonus money, they had proved their worth to the big bosses, yet again. After a few glasses, nature called, sensibly I decided not to risk the stairs in my heels. Right, before we go any further, can anyone, and I mean *anyone*, explain to me why so many venues that serve alcohol decide to have toilets up or down stairs? They might just as well push us over as soon as we walk through the door, Health and Safety where are you when it matters most??

Laughing At Myself

Anyway, rather than risk a tumble I nipped into the disabled cubicle. Once inside it took quite a wrestle to get the door closed enough to slide the lock over, But it wasn't until I sat down that it dawned on me, if the door had been that hard to close, that might translate into making it hard to open again.

The wine helped my mind cut out the middle-man of creating possible scenarios, and went straight to claustrophobic panic. Have you noticed my mind is helpful like that?

This time I tried to regulate my breathing, while I finished my pee and washed my hands – even panic shouldn't cancel out good hygiene practises. Then I discovered that yes, the lock would move, but the door wouldn't, it was firmly wedged in place. Pushing it didn't help, and it seemed like no-one could hear me hammering on the door over Edith Pilaf, and although it was a disabled toilet there was no emergency pull cord! I know right? (Again, Health and Safety I am calling you out on this one).

My heart was loud in my chest, despite the breathing exercises it still felt like the air was running out. My options were to try shoulder barging the door with all my might, to chew my way through it, or to give up and have a total melt down, sit and cry while waiting until closing time when the staff did the building checks. Or I could resign myself to living forever in a disabled toilet cubicle, but there isn't a great deal of nourishment in tissue paper.

Although naturally tempted by the later options I decided instead to go for a good old-fashioned shoulder to door barging. With all my might and extra adrenaline the previously wedged door flew open, and I went flying into the seated diners. As I shook myself off the manager sauntered by, grabbing him I explained in heated terms what had happened and waited for his expression of shock or apology.

All he said was 'oh yes, that door hasn't opened from the inside properly for weeks' and tottered off.

After that would you take any chances?

Death by Frisbee

Picture it, a festival on a burning hot summers day, music plays happily in the background. You are laughing with your friends, flirting, sunbathing, and after a few pints, dancing with abandon. When suddenly, SMACK! you take a heavy blow to the temple.

That's exactly what happened to me, during my perfect summer day, I got hit in the head by a rogue frisbee travelling at full speed. Eerily the music played on, but everything else within a ten foot radius stopped. People froze, presumably waiting to see if I would keel over, would I fall like a tree, straight over onto my face? or crumple on the spot? I stood very, very still and didn't react for a full minute. Doing an internal scan, I checked have I still got all my bits? have I got any extra bits? like a frisbee, protruding from my head? Yes, to the first, nope to the second, my head throbbed. Despite being stunned and hurt I was also mortified but didn't want to look like a total idiot.

Stupidly, I decided to try and style it out, this piece of genius involved standing straight, and staring into the crowd with a stupefied smile plastered to my face. It would be fair to say there was more work to do on how to appear casual.

People gathered around me, where had it come from? had it hurt? did I need help? The very attractive frisbee thrower came over to apologise, apparently, he hadn't noticed that there were people everywhere, had expected his friend to make the catch, blah, blah. After a few minutes of confirming there was no blood, and that I appeared not to have a brain injury the crowd dispersed and waited for the next entertainment.

All the caring attention somehow made it so much more embarrassing, so to distract myself and gather my thoughts, I said with a laugh, 'wasn't that hilarious?'. Giving my friends permission to ease the shock with some laughter felt like the best thing to do. After a few so typical of you comments, eye rolls and playful forehead slaps, their own not mine, we wandered over to a quiet bar to recover.

It was only once I bent down to flop onto a bean bag that I realised I was actually quite dizzy, and felt a little sick. In a strange twist we were all sober enough to know that we were over the drink drive

Laughing At Myself

limit, so wouldn't be able to go to the hospital. But we were all too inebriated to consider the first aid tent.

The World's Worst Burglar

Having locked myself out of my flat for maybe the tenth time in my life, and being exceptionally skint, I decided to try and get in without the aid of a locksmith. If you want to earn plenty of money in a job where people are always pleased to see you, and you don't mind getting called out at all hours, then locksmithing is the job for you.

It had been rushing to pick my sister Daisy up from the station that made me forget the keys. Luckily I'd also left a window open, and we managed to jiggle it down the frame, until it was just possible for me to fit through the gap.

However, before I could put my master plan into action I needed to get up onto the windowsill. Preparing to climb onto the skinny ledge, I was reminded why I never became a gymnast. Sadly, I was not blessed with co-ordination, or balance, and had very little

Laughing At Myself

head for heights. Luckily, with Daisy to stand below she would break my fall rather than the flower beds if it came to it. You may wonder why I didn't ask my sister to climb through instead of me? Firstly, I didn't think of it, and secondly being far more mature than me, she would have said no anyway.

So, all I had to do to save myself one hundred quid was lift myself up three feet onto a five centimetre strip of stone, and then climb, slide or fall through the open window onto the waiting sofa below. What could be easier? Not trying would have been easier, doing it without vertigo would have been easier, but we can't have everything.

Daisy gave me a hefty push from behind, and then lent into me, squishing me between her and the window. I managed to get onto the horizontal bar of the window superman style. Quite why I did this on my belly I cannot say.

A sudden out of body experience showed me just how ridiculous I looked, that started off a fit of the giggles that made it impossible to move. Daisy who was holding my legs up joined in, and our laughter echoed against the surrounding houses. It was only the urgency of the post giggle pee, that gave me the energy boost and courage to push myself through the window, and I landed with a flop on my sofa.

Eden Gruger

Being a particularly unadventurous type, this gave me the exhilaration that, I imagine, is only known by climbers of the Himalaya, swimmers of the channel, or the man who once walked a tightrope across Niagara Falls.

And, do you know, that despite all the noise and hullaballoo, not a single neighbour came to check what was going on? Something useful came of the experience though, in that I was able to knock another possible career off the list. There really isn't much call for such a loud burglar.

Mensa Test

At times I have tried to prove someone wrong by doing the biggest thing I can think of. Which is mainly daft, and hopefully something I will grow out of. It was being called stupid by someone who should have known better, that made me order a Mensa test. In case you weren't already aware, Mensa is an organisation whose membership is based on your having an IQ in the top 2% of the population. See what I mean, biggest thing I could think of, feel free to shake your head and roll your eyes.

Based on the result of the home test, I was asked to attend a centre to do the supervised one. No-one was more surprised than me I assure you, (although I hid it well, of course). Any opportunity to talk about the test was gratefully received or engineered. Did I rub the invite in at every chance? You don't even need to ask, you know I did.

To make sure that we weren't made late by traffic, getting lost or freak weather we left silly early, and then had two hours to waste. Would you believe that there wasn't a coffee shop anywhere? how on earth the people who lived nearby managed I have no idea.

Being one of those odd people who don't get worried about written exams, I hadn't expected to be nervous about this. But it didn't feel like any other test, this was different, for the first time I felt seriously intimidated. My stomach was in knots, imagining, no that's not it – expecting, that everyone else taking the test would be a genius (which is sort of the point I realise). In my mind's eye I saw them standing around discussing equations, or string theory (for all I know they are the same thing). They would have massive foreheads, clutch briefcases that they use as day bags, and everyone would be wearing a bow tie. As they arrived in ones and two's it was a relief to see that most people looked like me, and I could start to calm down.

Understandably, entry to such an exclusive group has some very strict rules. And many of those were about how the supervised test was carried out. The small, serious gentleman in charge explained all of the rules, in great detail, including how the questions would be asked, what you were and were not allowed to do once the question reading began and more, so much more.

Laughing At Myself

The very first thing that we had to do was put our age in years and months on our forms, this was used as part of the calculations to work out IQ. Then we handed them back, and small serious man carried on talking.

Mid whatever he was saying and barely a second before the first question was due to be asked, I realised that in my nerves I had made a mistake. With my heart pounding, I had to ask, in front of people who could potentially be the most intelligent in the country, if I could have my form back. The small, serious man looked confused, and asked why? Which forced me to admit that I had made an error. He asked what that was, and I had to say that I had written my age as thirty six and two months, rather than the forty one and five months that it actually was. Yet another time in my life when something that I thought was funny, was received as idiotic by those around me.

After all that when the results came back I hadn't even managed to prove my point, having gone through all that only to find out that I was in the top 6%.

The Countryside is/ not a Toilet

If you go to Italy, or in fact meet anyone Italian who tells you that England is a toilet, then I am sorry, it's time to hold my hands up, that is probably my fault. It's all because of a wild camping no amenities, boil your own water in a Billycan, Ordnance Survey Map trip that we took. Not my idea I promise you, but the things you do to impress a new partner are generally ridiculous.

It was one particularly unfortunate incident during this trip that led to my inadvertent ruining the reputation of the English countryside as far as Italy and the Italians are concerned.

Hardy I may not be, but I can pee in a bush with the best of them, so when nature called eventually there was no choice but to answer. There was quite a choice of 'facilities', a tree, some low bushes and a rock being the best options. Having chosen one of

Laughing At Myself

the bushes I unzipped, crouched, and tried not to pee on my boots (too much).

From around the sweeping bend appeared a group of ladies, so deep were they in their conversation that they wandered straight towards me utterly oblivious.

There was nothing I could do, being mid flow at this point, and not having the pelvic floor strength I once had. Giving a cough to alert them to my existence did nothing, and eventually the group nearly fell over me. I apologised – of course I did, how very English of me.

They looked embarrassed and said something to each other in Italian, let's assume it was 'my goodness, what a delight to meet you, we were just saying what a wonderful country you have, and we adore your Yorkshire puddings', although I may be wrong about that. As they backed away from me they managed to turn and catch an eyeful of my bloke, who was peeing against a tree, but in full view given their new angle.

I can only suspect that much of their holiday reminiscing to their friends, family, work colleagues and people they met, concerned how the English seem to use the countryside as one big toilet.

Sorry about that.

Flashing the Doctor

Since this happened, I have asked several friends and acquaintances this question. Most have looked at me blankly or with utter confusion, so let me ask you - if a doctor asked to listen to your chest, what would you do?

At my last check up the (attractive, young) locum asked to listen to my chest, and so instinctively and immediately I grabbed the hem of my jumper and raised it over my chin. Sign of a misspent youth?

'Oh' he said with a frown, which may have been in part the sight of my once white, now pinkish grey sports bra. It was clear that he was slightly shocked and not just by my failure to separate my washing. 'I was going to ask if you wanted a chaperone, but it's a bit late now'. 'No worries' I said putting my top down so he could call a receptionist. 'Anyway, Doctors have seen everything haven't they?'

Laughing At Myself

It wasn't until I met Marie for coffee later and told her the story that I started to wonder, she rolled her eyes at me, 'Well,' she said 'that's you a story for the poor lad, the middle aged woman who flashed her crinkly boobs at me today. Let's just hope that it hasn't made him rethink his whole career, we need more doctors not less'.

Cheeky cow, well, what would you have done?

I hope that you have enjoyed reading *Laughing at Myself*, and that it has left you wanting more, and if it has why not check out my other collections.

Down With Frogs is a collection of laugh out loud, hilarious, candid, occasionally tragic tales. It has always been said Princess' have to kiss a lot frogs before they find their Prince... so it makes sense that sometimes they might feel like giving up on love.

From awkward first meetings, dreadful dinners, to who should do the dusting, and sexual mishaps dating is a minefield.

The big question is will we learn from our mistakes or make them all over again?

Whether you are happily settled, or still looking, these laugh out loud, always candid, occasionally tragic tales will delight you.

Funny Bird shares some more of the darkly comic stories that make you laugh and cringe in equal measure. This mini collection for my Very Important Readers Group includes The Taxi Driver, Deafness and Accents, He is not Father Dougal and Chip pans and Louvre doors.

Friends Like These tells the laugh out loud stories of the good, the bad and the downright ugly friendships that we have through our lives. These hilarious, occasionally toe curling stories show how sometimes it's hard to tell the difference between a friend and an enemy.

You can follow me on social media, and subscribe to my Very Important Readers:

https://edengruger.com/eden-gruger-author
https://www.facebook.com/EdenGrugerTheAuthor
https://www.goodreads.com/author/show/18385919.Eden_Gruger

And don't forget I would really appreciate your leaving a review for this book!

https://edengruger.com/books
https://www.amazon.co.uk/Eden-Gruger/e/B093T6VHCV?
https://www.goodreads.com/author/show/18385919.Eden_Gruger

www.ingramcontent.com/pod-product-compliance
Lightning Source LLC
Chambersburg PA
CBHW071029080526
44587CB00015B/2554